OXFORD BOOKWORMS LIBRARY

Factfiles

Women Who Made a Difference

JANET HARDY-GOULD

Level 4 (1400 headwords)

Series Editor: Rachel Bladon
Acting Series Editor: Ruth Ballantyne
Editor: Madeleine Burgess

OXFORD
UNIVERSITY PRESS

Great Clarendon Street, Oxford, OX2 6DP, United Kingdom

Oxford University Press is a department of the University of Oxford. It furthers the University's objective of excellence in research, scholarship, and education by publishing worldwide. Oxford is a registered trade mark of Oxford University Press in the UK and in certain other countries

First published in Oxford Bookworms 2024

10 9 8 7 6 5 4 3

ISBN: 978 0 19 426780 9 Book
ISBN: 978 0 19 426777 9 Book and audio pack

For more information on the Oxford Bookworms Library, visit www.oup.com/elt/gradedreaders
Printed in China

ACKNOWLEDGEMENTS

Cover images by: Alamy (Album, Andrea Raffin, Archive PL, IanDagnall Computing, NASA Image Collection, The Chosunilbo JNS/Multi-Bits, Apic/Hulton Archive, Ben Stansall/AFP, Jemal Countess/WireImage, Anatolii Hordieiev)

The publisher would like to thank the following for their permission to reproduce photographs: Alamy (Jemal Countess/UPI, NASA Image Collection, World History Archive, Science History Images, Jimlop collection, History and Art Collection, Archive PL, Süeddeutsche Zeitung Photo, Casimiro, stockeurope); Album (EFE); Getty (Klaus Vedfelt/Digital Vision, Tim Whitby, Malin Hoelstad/SVD/TT/AFP, Carsten Koall, Maja Hitij, Ben Stansall/AFP, Heritage Images/Hulton Archive, Paul S. Howell/Hulton Archive, The Asahi Shimbun, Space Frontiers/Hulton Archive, Boyer/Roger-Viollet, AFP, Culture Club/Hulton Archive, Photo 12/Universal Images Group, Popperfoto, The Chosunilbo JNS/Multi-Bits, Pool – David J. Phillip, Cameron Spencer, Jemal Countess/Getty Images for Time Inc., Jasper Juinen, Bettmann, Darleen Rubin/WWD/Penske Media, Hulton-Deutsch Collection/Corbis, Frank Diernhammer/WWD/Penske Media, Austrian Archives/Imagno, Keystone-France/Gamma-Rapho, Chris Ware/Keystone Features/Hulton Archive, Andreas Rentz, Rose Hartman/Archive Photos, Robert Mitra/Penske Media, Tullio M. Puglia, Hulton Deutsch/Corbis Historical, Keystone-France, AFP PHOTO/Jim Watson); Shutterstock (Angelina Bambina, Hanna Franzen/EPA-EFE, Action Press, Shutterstock, Penta Press, sky vectors, Universal History Archive/UIG/Shutterstock, Ned Snowman, DFLC Prints)

CONTENTS

Introduction

If someone asked you to think of a woman who has 'made a difference', who would you choose? Would you choose a scientist, an artist, a writer, or a campaigner? Or perhaps a woman who does another kind of work? What do you think is so special about her?

Of course, there are billions of women in the world, and every one of them changes it in some way. So, in this book, what do we mean by 'made a difference'? When someone makes a difference, they make the world a better place for thousands or even millions of people. They do this by bringing big and important changes to the lives of others – in their community, in their country, or all around the world – often inspiring people to follow in their footsteps.

Each of the nine chapters in this book is about one woman who made a difference in this way. Women are the subject of this book because they have often had challenges or difficulties which have not always been problems for men in the same way. Also, the achievements of women have not always been as well-recognized as those of men.

Of course, there are many women from the past and present who could be in this book. But these nine women were chosen because they have each taken interesting and very different paths through life. They are all from different countries and moments in history, too, showing that women have always made, and continue to make, important changes all across the world.

The women in this book all had very varied lives and achieved different things, but one thing was the same for all of them: they were very determined about what they wanted to do, and when they met challenges or problems, they did not stop. They were brave and fearless, and they continued working for change even when it was very difficult. Over many years, they each followed their dreams and plans, and in the end, they made a big difference to the world. Here are their stories.

Note: In this book, we call the women by their last names, except for in chapter 3 (Marie Curie) and chapter 8 (Miuccia Prada). In these chapters, the women's first names are used because we also talk about other people in their families who have the same last name.

1 Greta Thunberg

WORK
Climate change campaigner

PLACE
Sweden

BORN
3rd January 2003

In 2018, Sweden was experiencing its hottest summer ever. Temperatures were much higher than usual, and the effects of these extreme weather conditions were everywhere. Forests were burning and over fifty fires were moving quickly across different parts of the country. Soon, the terrible fires were completely out of control and frightened families ran from their homes to escape the flames and thick smoke.

At home in Stockholm, a fifteen-year-old girl, Greta Thunberg, was following the news about the fires on social media. The situation was getting worse every day, and she began to feel extremely worried. But feeling like this was nothing new to Thunberg. From the age of eight, when most children are spending their time doing fun hobbies or playing sport, the young Thunberg had already started to learn about the dangers of climate change.

The effects of climate change across the world had become very clear in the years before 2018. Scientists had shown that the four years from 2013 to 2017 were the warmest ever. Sea levels had risen by 7.7 cm between 1993 and 2017, mostly caused by changes to the ice in very cold places like Antarctica. There had been a rise in the number of storms with very high winds, too, often in the US and the Caribbean. Thunberg saw these changes and became more and more angry that governments across the world were not doing enough to stop them. Now, Thunberg was seeing the frightening results of climate change in her own country, and she felt she *had* to do something.

In the late summer of 2018, Thunberg knew that national elections in Sweden were only weeks away, and that many important politicians would be in Parliament. She wanted to do something to remind these politicians about the extreme dangers of climate change. She also wanted to remind the Swedish government of the things that they had agreed to do in the 2015 Paris Climate Agreement. This important international agreement said that countries around the world had to work together to stop the world's temperature from rising too much.

So, on the evening of Sunday the 19th of August 2018, Thunberg made a sign – it said, 'School Strike For Climate' in Swedish. And the next morning, she started her strike. Instead of going to school, Thunberg went to the Swedish Parliament building. She sat down on the hard ground in front of the building with her sign next to her and a determined expression on her face. She stayed there all day, then returned the next morning, and the next. Over the following three weeks, Thunberg sat outside the Swedish Parliament in all kinds of weather. When people came to ask about her protest, she gave them information about climate change. Her message was simple: adults were destroying her future by doing nothing about climate change.

Thunberg outside the Swedish Parliament

By refusing to go to school, Thunberg was, of course, breaking the rules – she was not doing the things that she was supposed to do. But when people suggested that she should be in class, she had one thing to say: 'What am I going to learn in school?' she asked them. 'Facts don't matter any more, politicians aren't listening to scientists, so why should I learn?' Her parents did not agree with her refusal to go to school, but they understood her strong opinions about climate change. 'She can either sit at home and be really unhappy, or protest and be happy,' said her father.

Since Thunberg was very young, she had repeatedly explained the climate emergency to her family, and her parents had changed their daily lives because of this. They had followed Thunberg's example by not eating meat.

They had also stopped travelling by plane – and this was very difficult for Thunberg's mother as she was a world-famous singer who needed to travel abroad regularly for her job. These changes in her family's habits were important to Thunberg. If she could change the opinions and habits of her family, she thought, perhaps she could make a difference to the wider world, too.

Thunberg with her mother, 2018

Although Thunberg sat alone on the first day of her strike, news of her protest soon travelled. She put photos of her 'School Strike for Climate' on social media, and very soon climate campaigners began to 'like' and 'follow' her photos and messages. On the second morning, other people joined her protest, and after that more people joined every day. They were all inspired by this serious, determined girl with her big, clear sign.

As Thunberg's climate strike grew bigger, so did interest in it from around the world. News of her protest soon appeared on TV, on the radio, in newspapers, and on social media. And as news of her school strike travelled, people began to find out more about her. They learned that she was brave and ready to break the rules for what she believed in. They also learned that she is autistic. This means that she thinks, sees, and experiences the world differently to most other people, which can sometimes make life more challenging. But Thunberg says that being autistic helps her to study the things that interest her very carefully. So, it has helped her to understand the extreme dangers of climate change and how important it is to tell others about it.

After the Swedish elections ended in September 2018, Thunberg went back to school. However, she was determined not to stop her protest and continued her climate strike on Fridays, calling these days 'Fridays for Future'. She put messages on social media asking other students to strike as well. 'Sit outside *your* parliament or local government!' she told young people around the world. By December 2018, more than 20,000 young people in 270 towns and cities across the world had joined 'Fridays for Future'. For the first time ever, young people were regularly joining together in big numbers and telling politicians that they needed to do more about climate change.

A 'Fridays for Future' strike in Berlin, December 2018

In 2019, millions of people in different countries joined Thunberg in striking and protesting against climate change. For example, in February 2019, thousands of students walked through the streets of the Spanish city of Barcelona, with big crowds of noisy protesters filling large parts of the city centre. Everywhere you looked, there were colourful signs saying, 'Save Our Future', or 'Make The World Greta Again!' Protests were happening in different cities all over the world and sixteen-year-old Greta Thunberg sometimes led them herself, to the excitement of everyone there. Young people did not want to carry on waiting quietly for politicians to do something about climate change – they wanted something to happen now.

Thunberg leading a protest in Brussels, February 2019

In September 2019, the world saw the largest climate protest ever. Millions of people joined 2,500 protests in 163 different countries. In Germany, more than one million people filled the streets and stopped the traffic for hours. In Japan, students walked through Tokyo with signs saying 'Go Green!', 'Save The Earth', and 'Our House Is Burning!' And all these protests were inspired by Thunberg's Fridays for Future.

When Thunberg was in the news, Google searches for 'climate emergency' and other similar words rose steeply. People started to call this the 'Greta effect' – because of Thunberg, people were talking about climate change and the work that needed to happen. Many of the politicians in parliaments around the world listened to Thunberg, too. One British politician said, 'You have woken us up. We thank you. You have taught us all a really important lesson.'

But not every politician agreed with Thunberg. Some, like the Australian Prime Minister, Scott Morrison, argued that Thunberg was making young people feel too worried about climate change. Others just laughed at her. Some parents and teachers were angry with her for telling students not to go to school. But Thunberg argued back on social media and did not change her opinions.

Thunberg soon began to receive invitations to speak to important people about climate change, and she was welcomed inside parliaments across the world. She had developed a simple, honest, and angry way of speaking which was very different to the usual language of politicians. In front of the European Parliament in April 2019, she said loudly, 'It's OK if you refuse to listen to me. I am after all just a sixteen-year-old girl from Sweden. But you cannot [refuse to listen to] the scientists. Or the science. Or the millions of schoolchildren striking for the right to a future.'

Then, in the summer of 2019, Thunberg received perhaps her most important invitation yet. She was asked to speak about climate change to a large meeting of world leaders at the United Nations in New York in September. However, there was one difficulty – she had promised herself never to travel by plane, because flying is damaging for the climate. The only answer was to sail from Europe across the Atlantic by boat. The journey would not be easy: it was more than 3,000 miles and would take about two weeks, but Thunberg was determined not to fly.

So, on Wednesday the 14th of August 2019, Thunberg and her father left Plymouth in the UK on the *Malizia II*, an 18-metre-long sailing boat. It was different to most boats because it used the sun and waves to make the electricity that it needed during the voyage. It was a good way to travel for a climate change campaigner, but it was a difficult trip as the *Malizia II* was made for sailing fast, and there were no comfortable toilets or showers for the passengers.

Thunberg and her father took wonderful photos during the voyage, and put them on social media so the world could follow their journey. The third day on the boat was a Friday, so Thunberg stood on top of the boat with her 'School Strike For Climate' sign. High above her on the big, black sail, you could see the words #FridaysforFuture. By taking this long, tough journey across the Atlantic, Greta was showing how strongly she felt about the need for us all to fight climate change, and proving that people can do things that seem almost impossible in order to help.

Just over two weeks after it left the UK, the *Malizia II* arrived in New York on the 28th of August 2019, and Thunberg was welcomed by a large group of excited school students. They spoke to reporters about how

Thunberg sailing to New York, August 2019

Thunberg's extraordinary example had made them become climate campaigners. 'She's not afraid of anyone,' one fifteen-year-old boy said. 'She just wants to get her message out there. And she's willing to do anything for that. She's willing to cross the Atlantic for fifteen days on a small boat to do that. That just shows you how determined she is.'

Thunberg walked onto the stage at the United Nations in New York on the 23rd of September 2019. Presidents, world business leaders, and climate specialists sat in front of her. They were all very interested in what this famous girl was going to say. However, she did not start with a polite 'thank you' for the invitation to speak. Thunberg began at once with a serious message to the world leaders. 'This is all wrong. I shouldn't be up here. I should be back in school,' she cried. 'You have stolen my dreams and my childhood with your empty words.'

She argued that there was not enough serious action on the climate emergency, and she finished her talk by saying, 'Right here, right now is where we draw the line. The world is waking up. And change is coming, whether you like it or not!' Some of the people in the room shouted in agreement, but others looked uncomfortable. Sixteen-year-old Greta Thunberg had given one of the most determined and angry talks in the history of the United Nations.

Thunberg had started her work as a climate campaigner just over a year earlier when she sat alone outside the Swedish Parliament. She was unafraid to break the rules to achieve her goals, and her honest way of speaking and campaigning had inspired people and made them listen. In just twelve months, millions of young protesters had followed her call to march through their own towns and cities.

Climate change is still not being taken seriously enough and much more still needs to happen. But Thunberg started an important conversation and made people around the world take notice of the climate emergency. Through her actions she has made a big difference and continues to make a difference to this day.

Thunberg speaking at the United Nations, 23rd September 2019

2 Chiaki Mukai

WORK
Astronaut and doctor

PLACE
Japan

BORN
6th May 1952

It is the 12th of April 1961, and in Tatebayashi, a small city in Japan, a nine-year-old girl is listening to the news on the radio with great interest. The Russian astronaut Yuri Gagarin has just climbed into a spacecraft and flown high around the Earth, becoming the first person ever to travel into space. Like many others listening to the news that day, Chiaki Mukai was very excited by Yuri Gagarin's adventure. But this young girl did not imagine for a moment that she could ever follow his journey into space. At that time, the Japanese space programme was very small, and there were no Japanese astronauts at all, so the idea that Mukai could become an astronaut herself one day seemed impossible.

But the 1960s were a very exciting time for anyone who was interested in space. This was because of the famous 'space race' between the Soviet Union (which was made of Russia and many other countries) and the US, with both nations trying to be the first to explore space.

An early NASA moon lander in the 1960s

However, Mukai did not live in the Soviet Union or in the US. So, instead of thinking about going into space, she looked closer to home when she was planning what to do with her life. Her younger brother had an unusual bone disease, and when Mukai saw how doctors at the hospital had helped him and solved some of his health problems, she decided that she, too, wanted to work in medicine. Perhaps she could become a great doctor like the ones who had helped her brother.

At that time, only 10% of Japanese doctors were women, but Mukai was determined, and after years of study, she finally became a doctor of medicine in 1977. She then went on to train as a specialist doctor and started to work with people who were having problems with their hearts. In 1983, at the age of only thirty-one, Mukai became a leading university teacher in medicine at Keio University, in Tokyo.

Her work as a doctor was even more successful than she had dreamed of as a child. But in that same year, something happened that changed the path of Mukai's life. She was quietly drinking a cup of coffee after a hard night's work at the hospital when she noticed an interesting story in the newspaper. The Japanese government was looking for Japanese scientists to do research on one of the US Space Shuttles, which were spacecrafts used to make repeated journeys between Earth and space.

Mukai was very surprised. She had never imagined that there could be a chance for Japanese people to go on a mission into space. She immediately felt enthusiastic about the idea of becoming an astronaut herself. 'This is my chance to see my hometown and Earth [from space] with my own eyes!' she thought. As well as being excited by the thought of space travel, Mukai also saw that she could do research into the effects of being in space on the human body. She said later, 'I was always interested in solving [difficult problems] so when the Japanese government wanted somebody willing to go into space to do science experiments, I was really interested.'

Mukai contacted the government about joining the space programme, then she began to work hard on her fitness levels and English language abilities. Every day, she went swimming or spent hours studying because she wanted to have the best possible chance of getting a place on the mission. After all this hard work, in 1985, there was wonderful news: Mukai had been chosen to train for a shuttle mission in 1988! 533 Japanese men and women had tried to get a place to train for the mission, and she was one of only three successful people.

Mukai soon began her basic astronaut training. In this training, she needed to learn many difficult and important things. For example, she had to know how to survive in an emergency in space. She also learned how to live in the unusual conditions of space, and how to check all the controls on the spacecraft. She studied the stars, the Moon, and outer space, and learned other languages in order to speak to the international astronauts.

Mukai doing her astronaut training

But four months after Mukai began her training, there was some terrible news. The US Space Shuttle Challenger had exploded, only seventy-three seconds after leaving the ground. All seven astronauts on the shuttle were killed, and some were Mukai's friends. One of the astronauts who died, Christa McAuliffe, was a school teacher, and millions of people around the world had been following her journey. It was an awful accident.

Mukai felt very shaken, and she seriously thought about leaving the space programme because of the dangers involved. She wondered if it was time to return to her usual life as a doctor. But in the end, after many hours of careful thought, Mukai bravely decided to stay and follow her plan. She was determined to go into space one day, and nothing could change that.

Mukai was very hopeful about going on the 1988 space mission, but sadly it was delayed until 1992. She also knew that only one of the three Japanese astronauts who were training could go on this mission. After years of waiting, Mukai learned that she had not been chosen to go on the

1992 mission – a Japanese man called Mamoru Mohri was given the place. It was very disappointing news, but Mukai said to herself, 'It can't be helped. It isn't my time.' She decided not to spend too long thinking about this great disappointment. Instead, she began a new job helping the space mission from Earth – determined to learn as much as possible from her new work.

But Mukai did not have to wait much longer. Soon after, she was chosen from twenty-two people to be an astronaut on a space mission planned for 1994. After nearly ten years of hard work and waiting, Mukai's time had come at last! On the 8th of July 1994, she boarded the Space Shuttle Columbia at the NASA Kennedy Space Centre in the US. Like all the other astronauts on the Space Shuttle, Mukai needed to get into the spacecraft early, and lie on her back in her seat for several hours while the engineers did their final checks. After a long wait, the engines started with a loud noise, and the shuttle began to shake. It was ready to leave the Earth – the most dangerous part of any space mission. Several moments later, Mukai was pushed back hard into her seat. She was finally going into space!

Mukai going into space on the Space Shuttle Columbia, 8th July 1994

It was a big step for Mukai, but it was also a very important moment in the history of space travel. At the age of forty-two, she was not only the first Japanese woman to go into space, she was also the first Asian woman to go there, too. People across Japan felt delighted when they saw her on TV. She was also the only woman in the team of seven astronauts on the shuttle.

Mukai in space, July 1994

From space, Mukai looked down at the Earth and towards her hometown of Tatebayashi thousands of kilometres below. She was excited to finally be among the stars and felt proud to see the beautiful sight of the Earth from space. This space mission was also important because it was one of the longer NASA missions, and the astronauts did over eighty experiments on their dangerous journey high above the Earth. Mukai was responsible for many of the experiments on the mission, including some valuable research into the effects of space travel on the human body.

When Mukai landed safely back on Earth on the 23rd of July 1994, she had spent fifteen days in space, travelled 9.8 million kilometres, and gone around the Earth 236 times!

During the mission, Mukai had shown that she was an excellent space scientist and astronaut, so four years later, NASA invited her to join another important mission. This time it was a nine-day trip on the Space Shuttle Discovery which would also involve doing a lot of experiments. When the shuttle left the ground on the 29th of October 1998, Mukai became the first Japanese person to go into space twice, and once again she was the only woman in the team.

Mukai wanted to use the mission to interest young people in science and space. So, for one of her experiments, she planted vegetables on the space shuttle, and 6,000 Japanese school children planted vegetables on Earth at the same time. The students measured how well the plants were growing on Earth and wrote down their results. Mukai did the same for the plants growing in space. These results were then studied carefully to see how things grow differently in space. One of the students said that it was really exciting to think that the results could one day be helpful in growing food when people start living on space stations.

Mukai doing experiments on the Space Shuttle Discovery, 1998

After the mission, Mukai returned to her hometown of Tatebayashi where she was enthusiastically welcomed. Everybody wanted to shake her hand, and she met hundreds of local children. Some of them had made a special flag which she had taken on the mission, and she proudly returned it to them. She also answered questions from the children about her experiences in space and the science experiments that she had done.

One subject that interests many people is Mukai's opinion on women and equality. Her journey in life has been very unusual for a woman who grew up in the 1950s and 1960s, when there were very few women in space. But Mukai says that she never thinks about people being different because of their gender. She believes that the varied life experience of people in a team is much more important. Interestingly, she has said, 'I never thought there was anything I couldn't or shouldn't do because I'm a woman.'

When Chiaki Mukai became the first woman astronaut in her home country of Japan and also in Asia, she made a big difference to millions of other women, inspiring them to think about different paths in life. At last, they could see someone like them in space! Her journey was not easy, with disappointments and challenges along the way, but she remained determined and always made the best of difficult situations. She has always believed in people following their own dreams and one of her favourite ideas is, 'If you can dream it, you can do it!'

3 Marie Curie

WORK
Scientist

PLACE
Poland and France

BORN
7th November 1867

DIED
4th July 1934

Today, doctors all around the world use modern radioactive treatments to help some of the most seriously ill patients. The treatments that doctors use are new, but the ideas behind them are not. They were developed over a century ago by the scientist Marie Curie, who changed the world of medicine through her extraordinary work. But what did she discover and how did she achieve this, at a time when there were very few women in science?

At the end of the nineteenth century, Marie Curie was studying at university in Paris, France. At this time, many scientists were becoming interested in rays. Little was known about them, although two scientists had recently made important discoveries. In 1896, French scientist Henri Becquerel had found that a type of narrow ray, which was later called radioactivity, came from an element called uranium. And German scientist Wilhelm Roentgen had discovered 'X-rays' in 1895, which doctors could use to see inside people's bodies.

X-ray of Roentgen's wife's hand

Men and women around the world were extremely excited by Roentgen's wonderful discovery and his very first X-ray. However, Marie was more interested in Becquerel's discovery of the rays from radioactive uranium. So in 1896, while she was still at university, she began to study pitchblende. Pitchblende is a type of radioactive rock that comes from deep under the ground in some places. Scientists already knew that pitchblende contained uranium, but Marie felt that there could be more interesting things to learn about it. Perhaps pitchblende even contained another element. Other scientists at the time doubted her ideas. 'What does this young woman know about new elements?' they asked. The challenge for Marie was to prove them wrong, but luckily, meeting challenges and solving problems were not new to this young scientist.

Marie Curie was born in Poland with the name Maria Skłodowska. She was the youngest of five brothers and sisters, and both of her parents were teachers. Her father's employment situation was uncertain, and he often had to move from job to job, while the family lived in smaller and smaller apartments. When Maria was eleven, her mother and one of her older sisters both died, leaving Maria deeply sad.

After leaving school a few years later, Maria dreamed of going to university. However, at that time, women in Poland were not allowed to study at a higher level than school. She knew that women could go to university in France, but that would be difficult for her. Her family did not have a lot of money, and students in France needed to pay for their lessons and, of course, pay for food and somewhere to live.

Maria (left) with her father and sisters

But Maria was determined, so she made a special arrangement with her sister, Bronya. First, Maria would work in Poland to help pay for Bronya to study at university in Paris. Later, at the end of her studies, Bronya would earn money in Paris to help pay for Maria to go to university. If the plan was successful, both sisters would receive the university education that they desperately wanted. It was an early example of Maria's intelligent problem-solving which was so important later in her work.

After six long years of studying, Bronya finally left university in Paris and became a doctor. Then, in 1891, Maria came to Paris to begin her studies in science at the Sorbonne – one of the top universities in France. Their plan had worked, and now Maria was following her dream of going to university!

When she arrived in Paris at the age of twenty-four, Maria changed her name to Marie because it sounded more French. Perhaps she also thought that it would help people to accept her more in France. Her new life was extremely hard at first. She was living in a small, cold room at the top of an old building in a student neighbourhood. The room had no hot water or heating, and it was so cold at night that she had to put on a lot of clothes in order to get to sleep.

The conditions at the university were not easy either. Marie had grown up speaking Polish, but her new classes were all in French, so she needed to work very hard to understand everything. There were also very few students who were women at the time, and some people felt that men had more right to be at the university than women. Although there were many challenges during Marie's early years at the Sorbonne in Paris, she loved the freedom to study and do experiments. 'It was like a new world opened to me, the world of science, which I was at last [allowed] to know,' she later explained. She also achieved something extraordinary. Marie came top of her physics class – and was given money to continue her studies in science.

During these studies, in 1894, she met Pierre Curie, who was an internationally-known French scientist. They had very similar interests and fell in love. She had planned to return to Poland after university, but in the end, she decided to stay in France and marry Pierre. They soon had their

Marie in Paris, 1895

first child, a daughter called Irène, in 1897. Mothers at this time were usually expected to take care of their children at home, and not work or study. But Marie wanted to continue with her work, so she needed to find someone to look after Irène. Again, she was able to solve this problem by thinking and doing things differently. It was very unusual for a man to care for children at this time, but the Curies bought a house with Pierre's father, who had been a doctor, and he looked after Irène, as well as the Curies's second daughter, Ève, who was born later.

Marie with her new husband, Pierre Curie

It was around this time that Marie Curie began to try to find the mysterious new element in pitchblende. If she was successful, it would be an important achievement. Scientists who discover new elements often become very famous for their work. When Marie was born in 1867, scientists only knew about sixty-three elements. By 1900, more than eighty had been discovered, and today we know of 118. So Marie was working at a time when lots of new elements were being discovered, and she hoped to find one herself.

Pierre asked to join Marie in her important work, and in 1898, they believed they had found not one new element in pitchblende, but two! These elements were polonium, which they named after Poland, Marie's homeland, and radium, which they named after the word 'ray'. In Marie's reports about the new elements, she introduced the word 'radioactive' to the scientific community for the first time. She believed that radium could be a very important element, as she thought that it was much more radioactive than uranium. However, she first needed to separate some radium and polonium from the pitchblende to prove to other scientists that these new elements were real. Pitchblende contains around thirty elements, so it was going to be very difficult to find and separate the radioactive ones.

Pierre asked the Sorbonne University for a special place where they could work with pitchblende, but the only room available was a dirty, old building behind the School of Physics. It had a glass roof and was extremely hot in the summer and absolutely freezing in the winter. After visiting the Curies there, the famous scientist Wilhelm Ostwald said that he thought it looked like a place for keeping horses or potatoes! It was very challenging to work there, but that did not stop the Curies from doing their important experiments.

Marie began separating the different parts of pitchblende by heating it with other things. She often worked with 20 kilograms of pitchblende at a time, putting everything together in a large pot. She then moved it around with a long, metal bar which was nearly as tall as she was. She later said that she was almost broken with tiredness at the end of each day, but after more than three years of painful work, Marie separated out one tenth of a gram of radium from the pitchblende. She had finally shown that radium was a real element.

Marie working on radioactive elements, 1906

Polonium was even more difficult to work with and Marie never managed to completely separate it from the other elements in pitchblende. However, Marie was still named as the discoverer of polonium because she had begun the work of finding it. She later explained what she had discovered to the top physics teachers and researchers at the university, and received the highest level of degree for her work. She was the first ever woman in French history to receive one of these types of degree. The university teachers said that the results of her experiments were the greatest discoveries in a higher-level science degree of this type. She had discovered something very important, and she was challenging ideas about women in science, too.

The Curies began to give talks about the newly discovered radium. They had great hopes that doctors could use it in the treatment of very serious illnesses in the future. This was important, as there were not many treatments in the early 1900s. The Curies were right, and in time, Marie Curie's discoveries have made a very big difference to the world of medicine, helping millions of very ill people to get better.

However, the fact that radium was so radioactive meant that it could also have terrible effects on people who worked with it. Both Marie and Pierre often felt extremely tired or unwell, and the ends of their fingers went black and never returned to their normal colour. The radioactivity stayed on their things, too. Some of Marie's notes are kept in special boxes to this day because they are still so radioactive.

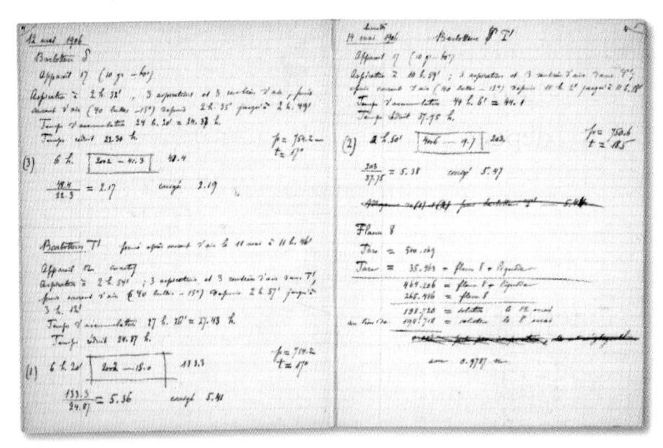

Marie's notebook

In 1903, the most important group of French scientists suggested that Pierre Curie and Henri Becquerel should win the Nobel Prize in physics for their work. At this time, it was expected that scientists who made great discoveries would be men, and Marie's name was not mentioned at all. When Pierre learned about this, he said that Marie must receive the prize as well – her ideas and research had been at the heart of everything that had been achieved.

So in December 1903, Marie Curie and her husband were both given the Nobel Prize for their research on radioactivity, along with Henri Becquerel. It was a truly important moment. Marie had become the first woman in history to receive a Nobel prize. Later, in 1911, she was given a second Nobel prize for the discovery of radium and polonium, becoming the first person ever to win two Nobel prizes. She is also the only person to receive a Nobel prize in two different sciences.

Marie Curie's hard work and ability to solve problems and meet challenges led to her extremely important achievements in the world of science. Over the years, her work has made an extraordinary difference to other scientists who have built on her ideas, and she has inspired women who want to study and work in science. Her discoveries have become central to the world of medicine, too. All treatments that use radioactivity depend on her work. For these reasons, Marie Curie is one of the most important figures in the history of science.

Marie working at her desk, 1910

4 Yuna Kim

WORK
Figure skater

PLACE
South Korea

BORN
5th September 1990

It is the start of the 2018 Winter Olympics in PyeongChang, South Korea. A young woman is standing on a small ice rink high above the large crowd. Her name is Yuna Kim, or 'Queen Yuna' to the many people who love her. In her long, white dress, she starts to skate to beautiful music while the crowd looks up at her with excitement. After a few moments, she pauses, and two people skate over to her. They carefully pass her the famous Olympic flame, and Yuna Kim uses it to light a fire next to her. Everyone watches the fire as it travels to the Olympic bowl high in the air. The PyeongChang 2018 Winter Olympics are open at last!

Yuna Kim is a world-famous figure skater and an extremely popular person on TV and social media in South Korea, with over one million people following her. She also played a very important part in bringing the 2018 Winter Olympics to South Korea. But she had a long and difficult journey to get to that Olympic ice rink.

Kim opening the PyeongChang Winter Olympics, 9th February 2018

Yuna Kim started figure skating lessons at the age of six. Her first trainer could see that she was unusually good at the sport, and he even said to her mother that Yuna Kim would become one of the world's greatest figure skaters one day! However, it was difficult to learn figure skating in the 1990s in South Korea because it was not a popular sport. 'During my early skating years,' Kim later explained, 'there were not many ice rinks in Korea.' There were not any real skate shops either, so Kim sometimes had to train in skates that did not fit her feet well. These often hurt and sometimes made it difficult to skate. But these problems did not stop her from continuing with the sport that she had grown to love.

One day, at the age of seven, Kim saw something on TV which had a big effect on her life. 'When I had just started figure skating, I discovered the Olympics by watching Nagano [in Japan] 1998,' she later told reporters. 'At that time, I didn't know what the Olympics were. I just saw the international sportspeople standing on this big stage, and said, "Wow that's cool! I want to be there."'

Kim began to figure skate for long hours with her trainers, determined to learn new and difficult jumps and turns, and become faster and stronger. She thought, perhaps, that if she trained hard, she could achieve her dream of going to the Olympics. She started to enter figure skating championships, and in 2003, at the age of twelve, she became the youngest ever skater to win the South Korean National Championships – an extraordinary achievement. She had success in other countries, too, and in 2009, she made history at the World Championships by bringing home South Korea's first international figure skating gold medal.

She managed to achieve her childhood dream when she was chosen to figure skate at the Winter Olympics in Vancouver, Canada in 2010. As the world figure skating champion, everyone in South Korea was expecting her to do extremely well. It was wonderful that so many people at home thought she could win, though Kim was worried that she would disappoint them.

Kim arrived in Vancouver with her trainer several days before the games started. Instead of staying at the Olympic Village with the other skaters, she went to a basic hotel nearly 20 kilometres away. Here, she could prepare for her important moment without any TV reporters. While Kim was there, one of her trainers noticed something interesting – although her first Olympics were now only days away, Kim looked strong and completely in control. No one could doubt her courage, as she calmly prepared for her first Olympic Games at the age of only nineteen.

On the 23rd of February 2010, Kim stood on the edge of the ice at the Olympic rink with South Korean flags waving behind her in the crowd. And in towns and cities across South Korea and all over the world, millions of people watched on their TV screens. As soon as Kim started skating, people held their breath. Her routine was extraordinary – it was fast, exciting and beautiful, and she skated to a famous song from a *James Bond* film. The crowd loved it, and the judges gave her the highest number of points ever – which put her five points ahead of the skater in second place. It was a wonderful start, and the result of years of hard work.

In order to win the gold medal, Kim still needed to skate perfectly in her final routine two days later. On the 25th of February, Kim went on to skate one of the best routines of her life. It was extremely difficult, with dangerous jumps and high speed, but Kim skated beautifully to the music. The judges again gave her the highest number of points ever for a routine of this type.

Kim skating at the Olympics, 23rd February 2018

Later that day, Kim stood high on the Olympic platform with flowers in her hand and the national music of South Korea playing loudly in her ears. Her first trainer had been right – she had become the best figure skater in the world and had won an Olympic gold medal to prove it. She had also made her nation proud by becoming the first ever South Korean to win an Olympic figure skating medal.

Kim immediately returned to South Korea, where she was welcomed by the president. She was now a superstar both at home and abroad. People loved her, and she had made the sport of figure skating more popular across South Korea, too – inspiring others to try it. The sport had been almost unknown in her country when she started, but her success changed this. 'When I was young, many people didn't know what figure skating was,' she later said. 'Some who knew of it thought of it as dancing on ice. But as I entered international (championships) and got good results, many people got to know more about it.' Kim became one of *Time* magazine's top 100 people in the world that year – these people are chosen because they are changing the world through their achievements.

Kim had already done so much at a very young age, but she wanted to keep going and achieve more. In 2011, she was invited to join the South Korean Olympic bid team for the 2018 Winter Olympics and become 'the face of PyeongChang'. She enthusiastically agreed to help. The team had seen that Kim was hard-working, determined, and popular, and they hoped that this could help to win the bid. South Korea had been hoping to have the Winter Olympics for a long time. However, there had been earlier disappointments when they failed to win bids for both the 2010 and the 2014 Winter Olympics, and those games happened in other countries. South Korea's hopes were now high that their third bid would be successful.

A visit by the International Olympic Committee to PyeongChang in February 2011 had gone well and the Olympic visitors had noted two important things. Winter sports had become better and more popular in South Korea, and South Koreans seemed extremely enthusiastic about having the games there, too. There is little doubt that Yuna Kim's international success over the years had helped to make these differences. And these changes made South Korea's bid much stronger than it had been before.

In July 2011, Kim travelled with the South Korean Olympic bid team to Durban in South Africa, where the International Olympic Committee were meeting to decide where the 2018 Winter Olympics were going to happen. They were considering bids from three countries: France, Germany and, of course, South Korea. Kim and her team needed to give an important talk and persuade the Committee that PyeongChang in South Korea was the best possible place to hold the Winter Olympics. Kim was very serious about her part, and she did everything that she could to help win the bid. She wrote about the South Korean bid in a South African newspaper, and she gave a skating lesson to twelve young South African figure skaters. But most importantly, she sat in her hotel room for hours, carefully reading aloud the talk that she was going to give to the International Olympic Committee in her excellent English. She read it again and again in the same way that she had worked determinedly on her skating routines.

When Kim finally stood in front of the International Olympic Committee, she showed great courage, spoke confidently, and gave a perfect talk. Her dream of bringing the Winter Olympics to South Korea shone through her words. At the end of all the bids from the three different countries, there was no need for a second vote by the people in the International Olympic Committee. PyeongChang won the Olympic bid immediately with sixty-three of the ninety-five votes. Kim had done it! She had made her country proud again by helping to win their Winter Olympics bid. When asked, almost half of South Koreans thought that Kim had played the main part in winning the bid.

Kim waving at the International Olympic Committee in Durban, 6th July 2011

In 2018, when Yuna Kim finally opened the Winter Olympics, the first person to hold the Olympic flame on its journey to PyeongChang was a South Korean figure skater called You Young. She was the youngest ever winner of the South Korean National Championships at the age of eleven and was now a successful world figure skater, who had been inspired by Kim's example. 'Yuna Kim made me start figure skating when I was young because I really liked watching her in Vancouver,' You Young later explained.

Yuna Kim's natural ability, determined character, courage, and hard work helped her to reach the top of her sport and become the first South Korean person to win an Olympic figure skating medal, inspiring many others, like You Young, to do new and difficult things. As a result of her example, she helped to make figure skating and other winter sports popular in her country. She also played an important part in bringing the Winter Olympics home to South Korea. For all these reasons, she became known as 'Queen Yuna', a truly special person at the heart of her nation.

5 Frida Kahlo

WORK
Artist

PLACE
Mexico

BORN
6th July 1907

DIED
13th July 1954

Frida Kahlo was an extraordinary artist who explored her own identity through art. She challenged the way that women had traditionally been shown in paintings and refused to conform to the stereotypes of her time. During her life, she had some success as an artist, but it was only after her death that people understood the great importance of her work, and how she had changed the world for women and art. Now she is a very famous artist – but how did she start her journey of exploring herself through art? And what made her paint those unusual paintings?

In September 1925, when she was eighteen years old, Kahlo was in a serious bus crash while on the way home from school. In the terrible accident, a metal bar went through her body, and many of the bones in her feet, back, and legs were broken. Kahlo nearly died, and she had to lie in bed for months at *La Casa Azul*, her family home in Coyoacán, Mexico City. The accident changed everything for Kahlo: before, she had wanted to become a doctor; after, she knew that she could no longer follow this dream because her health was not good enough.

Kahlo had been interested in art from an early age, so one day, while she was in bed after the accident, her father lent her some of his paints and brushes. Her mother bought her a wooden holder to keep paper in front of her in bed, and Kahlo asked for a large mirror to go on top of this. This helped her to see herself easily. Kahlo now began to paint in bed – sometimes trying self-portraits using the big mirror. She later explained her lifelong interest in self-portrait painting and why she used herself as a subject for paintings. 'I paint myself because I am often alone,' she said. 'And I am the subject I know best.'

Kahlo began to think that becoming an artist could one day be possible, although it would not be an easy path. Most well-known artists at that time were men, and it was often difficult for women to get training or have their own art shows.

Kahlo in 1926

Self-Portrait in a Velvet Dress, 1926

This was Kahlo's first self-portrait and it shows her wearing a dark red dress. *Self-Portrait in a Velvet Dress* gives one of the first examples of Kahlo's famous 'stare'. In traditional paintings, women are often looking down, or away from the viewer, but Kahlo shows herself staring calmly and confidently out of this picture. Anyone looking at the painting is immediately pulled towards Kahlo's strong face, brown eyes, and thick eyebrows, as well as the light moustache above her lips.

Search for this painting online and do the same for Kahlo's other paintings that are described.

Kahlo chose to paint herself in this way to make people stop and think. She was challenging traditional ideas of beauty, which was an extremely unusual thing to do at this time – when most paintings of women were by men, and showed women in a stereotypically pretty way. But Kahlo was doing something different. She was refusing to pretend to be perfect and was not afraid to show herself as she really was.

Today, there are lots of photos of people looking perfect on social media, and this can sometimes make people feel that they need to change how they look, or hide the things that make them different or unusual. Although *Self-Portrait in a Velvet Dress* was painted years before social media began, Kahlo's painting inspires us to rethink what is beautiful, and her work still gives an important message today – it is acceptable to be yourself and to look different to other people.

Kahlo refused to conform to other stereotypes in art, too. For example, she returned to the idea of her own pain again and again in her paintings, because it was a subject that she understood very well. Kahlo unfortunately had poor health for most of her life, even before the bus crash. At the age of six, she had had a serious illness, which left one of her legs thinner than the other and gave her lifelong pain. It had also delayed her start at school, which made her feel separate from other children. As she grew older, Kahlo continued to experience more health problems and pain, which meant that she sometimes had to stay in hospital for a long time. However, she was determined to continue painting, although she could not sit or stand for very long.

By using her own life, with all its difficulties, problems, and fears, Kahlo never conformed to traditional ideas about what was or was not acceptable to paint, and she was not afraid to show personal moments of her life. She once said about her art, 'My painting carries with it the message of pain.' She was challenging the art world and changing our ideas about what artists can show or explore in their art.

The Bus, 1929

The Bus shows six very different passengers sitting next to each other on a bus. It is thought that the young woman on the right at the end is Kahlo herself. The painting shows the moment of calm just before her sudden accident in 1925.

In 1922, three years before her bus accident, Frida Kahlo met the famous Mexican artist Diego Rivera when he came to do a painting at her school. Many years later, in the late 1920s, their paths crossed again, and they fell in love and got married. Kahlo and Rivera had a very unusual marriage.

Unlike other couples at this time, they both worked, and they also recognized each other as artists. They learned from each other's painting abilities and ideas, too. However, they often argued and later had a house built in Mexico City which had two separate parts, one for her and one for him, joined by a bridge in the middle.

Kahlo with her husband, Diego Rivera

Kahlo and Rivera had similar ideas about the importance of traditional Mexican culture in a country where European or American culture was often seen as more important. Kahlo's father was European, but her mother was Spanish-Mexican, and Kahlo lived in Mexico for most of her life. From 1929, Kahlo began to explore the Mexican part of her identity, changing the way that she painted and dressed. Kahlo said, 'It is not possible to present ... [a] picture of our culture without all the voices of the people in the culture.'

Frida and Diego Rivera, 1931

The painting shows the couple not long after their wedding. They stand together hand-in-hand, staring out of the painting. Unlike in her earlier painting, *Self-Portrait in a Velvet Dress*, Kahlo is now wearing brightly coloured Mexican clothes and not the European clothes that were popular with some of her Mexican family and friends. The painting is also interesting because of its painting style. The subjects are much 'flatter' and are more similar to traditional Mexican paintings than European ones.

Fulang-Chang and I, 1937

This self-portrait was part of Kahlo's first and only art show in the US in 1938. It was the earliest of her self-portraits with animals and it shows her with her monkey, Fulang-Chang. The closeness between Kahlo and Fulang-Chang in the painting, and the varied Mexican plants behind her, show her love of nature and animals. The thick hair next to Kahlo's neck and on her face matches the 'hairy' plants behind her.

This painting perhaps shows us something else about Kahlo's personal life and pain. Kahlo and Rivera could not have children, and in this painting, Kahlo is holding the monkey in the same way that babies are held in old, Italian paintings. This was a brave thing to show in a picture at the time. This painting is also another example of how Kahlo explored the way that she looked, and refused to conform to traditional ideas of beauty, or how women should live and behave.

Kahlo became well-known for her Mexican clothes. Her style consisted of a half-circle of flowers in her hair and bright red lips, as well as a long, flowing Mexican skirt and a colourful top. When she travelled to other countries, people frequently came up to her and showed interest in her style, and she was partly responsible for making traditional Mexican clothes much more widely known abroad. Later in the 1930s, fashion designers also began to notice Kahlo's interesting style. In 1937, she appeared in the fashionable magazine, *Vogue*, and after she visited Paris in 1939, the famous French fashion designer Elsa Schiaparelli made a special dress named after her.

Kahlo wearing traditional Mexican clothes, 1944

Kahlo was not only interested in the clothes of Mexico, but also loved the wonderful nature in her country. Many of her paintings show the plants, flowers, and wild animals of Mexico. By choosing Mexican subjects and a traditional Mexican style in her paintings, Kahlo was challenging ideas about American and European culture being better. She was showing that Mexican culture is important, too, and she was helping to make Mexican art and artists more popular.

Kahlo's health continued to get worse and, in 1950, she had to spend nine months in hospital. Although she had serious health conditions, she was still involved in the world of art. In April 1953, Kahlo had her first art show in Mexico and it was a very important moment – it was now time for people in Mexico to see a large number of Kahlo's paintings.

Kahlo with her doctor, 1952

However, doctors warned that she was too ill to travel and that she absolutely had to rest. Kahlo was desperate to go, so in answer to this, she was taken on her large bed to the art show and spoke from there to the visitors at the show. 'I am not sick,' she said to the reporters who were there, 'I am broken. But I am happy to be alive as long as I can paint.'

Kahlo died in 1954 at the age of forty-seven. From the time of her accident in 1925 until her death, Kahlo made 143 paintings, of which fifty-five were self-portraits. These self-portraits were not well-known outside Mexico during her lifetime. However, since her death, her paintings have become more and more famous, and Kahlo is now one of the most studied and discussed artists in the world.

Frida Kahlo made a difference in many ways to many people. She painted herself in an honest and unusual style for her time, challenging stereotypes of women's beauty in art and in life. She also challenged ideas about what subjects artists could show, by exploring her own pain in her paintings, as well as her Mexican identity. In her life, in her marriage, and in her art, Kahlo always refused to conform or allow anything to stop her. Her work and ideas inspired other artists, too. It is partly because of Kahlo that what we see now in art is much more honest and interesting. She was ahead of her time, and this explains why she is still so popular today.

6 Maya Angelou

WORK
Writer, campaigner, actor, teacher

PLACE
The US

BORN
4th April 1928

DIED
28th May 2014

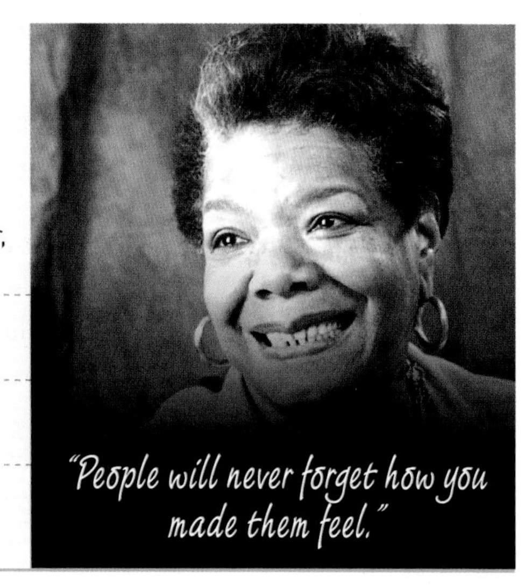

It is 2013. The American writer Maya Angelou stands in front of a meeting of ten thousand teachers in Chicago, in the US. People have been queuing for two hours to hear this famous woman speak, and there is not a single empty seat in the place. Angelou begins to talk about teachers – how they give hope, promise, and the possibility of change to their students. Without reading from notes, she speaks beautifully and amusingly about all the teachers in her life who have helped her to learn.

It was a wonderful talk by a natural storyteller. Angelou had a special way of making people want to listen to her. For over fifty years, she told stories about black people and about women. She told these stories in person, in her books, in poetry and plays, on screen, and later on social media. In her adult life, she spoke to many thousands of people and became very famous for her civil rights work, helping to bring big changes for black people in the US and beyond by describing their lives and experiences. Over the years, her words have reached millions of people and given hope to those whose voices are often not heard.

Angelou speaking about one of her books, 1978

However, in Angelou's early life, it seemed unlikely that she would ever use her voice to make a difference in this way. In 1936, when Angelou was only eight years old, she had a terrible experience. One day, her mother's boyfriend was very violent to her, and after this happened, Angelou stopped speaking. Her family tried to help her, but although she had been talkative in the past, she would not say a word. She was completely silent, and the months of silence soon became years.

Although Angelou did not speak, she loved reading and often visited the library in Stamps, Arkansas. This was the small town where she lived for much of her childhood with her grandmother, who owned a food shop. A local teacher, Mrs Flowers, knew about Angelou's love of books and wanted to help her speak again. Like Angelou, Mrs Flowers was part of the black community. But unlike many other people from that community, Mrs Flowers had been able to get a higher education and become a teacher.

Mrs Flowers helped Angelou by reading stories and poetry to her. Angelou liked this kind teacher, so she always listened carefully. Angelou's interest in reading grew, and Mrs Flowers introduced her to writers like Shakespeare, Dickens, and Edgar Allan Poe. After a long time spent reading together, Mrs Flowers one day challenged Angelou to read some poetry aloud, explaining that, 'You do not love poetry until you speak it.' At first, Angelou could not do it. But in the end, she slowly read aloud from a book of poetry and heard the words on the page come alive in her own voice. At the age of thirteen, after five long years of silence, Angelou had finally started to speak again.

During those silent years in Stamps, Angelou had developed an extraordinary ability to look and listen very carefully to the world around her, then remember everything that she had seen or heard. She began to notice and learn about the inequality experienced by black people, as well as women, in her own small town.

Like other towns in the south of the US at this time, Stamps was segregated, which meant that black families and white families had to live completely separately from each other. The black community lived in its own neighbourhood with its own schools and churches, separated from the richer, white community. Angelou later said that black children often did not know what white people looked like because the two communities were so segregated. It was even difficult for black people to receive medical help, because white doctors often refused to see them.

There were laws, too, which said that black people could not sit at the front of buses, only at the back. Thousands of white men in the US belonged to a secret group called the Ku Klux Klan, which was very violent to the black community. Angelou later said that she hated crossing the railway line to go from her home in Stamps to the white community, because she felt unsafe and afraid there. These early experiences showed Angelou that the world badly needed to change and become a better place for everyone. And perhaps this was when she began to have the idea that she could join the fight against this terrible inequality one day.

After spending much of her childhood in Stamps, Angelou left at the age of fourteen to go and live with her mother in San Francisco. Angelou enjoyed her new school and, because she always had stories that she wanted to tell, she often spent her free time writing. She later had a baby boy and became a single parent, living on her own with her son. As she needed to earn money to look after herself and her son, she did a variety of jobs, and these often changed as she became interested in new and different things. Over the years she was a cook, a dancer, then later an actor and a reporter. Her interesting and varied life gave her a deep understanding of many different ways of living, and this helped her in her writing.

Angelou moved to New York in 1959 when she was in her early thirties. She joined a group of writers and became friends with the well-known black writer James Baldwin. It was at this time that she first heard the famous civil rights campaigner Martin Luther King Jr. speak. He was a leader of the civil rights movement in the US, and he had been involved in important protests. Some of the goals of this movement were to get the same rights for black people as white people and to end racism, segregated communities, and violent crimes towards the black community.

Martin Luther King Jr. speaking to a large crowd

Angelou liked his ideas, his courage, and his extraordinary abilities as a speaker. She decided to join the civil rights movement, and became a close friend to both Martin Luther King and his wife. Angelou wanted to help stop the inequalities that she had seen between black and white people since childhood, and she was involved in the civil rights movement for many years.

But on the 4th of April 1968, something terrible happened. Martin Luther King was shot and killed in Memphis, Tennessee, by a man who was against King's ideas. Angelou was so sad that she stopped eating and refused to answer the phone. But her friend James Baldwin appeared at her front door one day and refused to leave until she agreed to come out with him. He took her to the home of the writer and artist Jules Feiffer and his wife Judy.

There were lots of interesting people at the Feiffers' home that night, and they started to tell stories about their childhoods. They spoke one by one, until at last, it was Angelou's time to speak. When she started talking, everyone listened in great surprise. Her story telling abilities and her life experiences were extraordinary. The next day, Judy Feiffer phoned a friend who managed an important book company and told him all about Angelou. He was very excited and asked Angelou to write an autobiography – a book about her own life – but she refused at first. She had written poetry and plays before, but never an autobiography. In fact, she refused three times before she finally accepted.

So Angelou shut herself away and began to write a book about her childhood that she later called *I Know Why The Caged Bird Sings*. As she wrote, Angelou tried to bring to life her experience as a black girl in a segregated town in the US. *I Know Why The Caged Bird Sings* tells of Angelou's early life from the ages of three to seventeen. She describes how she saw the effects of racism at her grandmother's shop in Stamps. For example, one night, her grandmother has to hide Angelou's Uncle Willie in a vegetable box so that he can avoid the Ku Klux Klan, who are looking for a black man to hurt. She also tells how three white girls make fun of her grandmother outside her shop. Angelou gets very angry, but she sees her grandmother proudly refuse to reply to the cruel things that the girls say. In the end, Angelou realizes that her grandmother has won because she has remained strong and calm in this difficult situation.

In the book, young Angelou moves from being the subject of racism, for example, when she is refused treatment for toothache because of the colour of her skin, to becoming a self-confident young woman at the end. There is, of course, a place in the book for her teacher, Mrs Flowers, and the help that she gave Angelou with speaking and reading. And it is clear in the book that Angelou's love of reading was very important in helping her to survive the racism and difficulties that she experienced.

When the book appeared in 1969, it was an immediate success. Angelou had managed to find her own innovative autobiographical style, which was conversational and invited the reader to join her world and learn its secrets. People became very interested in this personal story, and it was one of the first books to show the real life of a young black girl and her family and the racism that they met.

Angelou in 1970

For millions of people, Angelou had done something very special and important with this book. For some, it gave a view into a different world. For the black community in the US and black women, it finally told part of their story, inspiring many of them to tell their own. The book stayed on the bestseller list for two years and sold over one million copies. It later appeared in seventeen different languages and was made into a film. It is still studied today by school and university students across the world.

Angelou went on to write six other autobiographies covering her whole life. She also worked at a university for many years, where she taught about books and writing, and called herself 'a teacher who writes'. Like Mrs Flowers, Angelou enriched the lives of her students by helping them to discover their own ways of speaking and writing.

Maya Angelou made a very big difference to the cultural identity of her country. As a child, she could not speak, but she found her voice again through reading. As an adult, many millions of people listened to her as she talked about her own story, and the stories of other people who do not have equality. She helped to start a conversation about difficult subjects like racism and identity, and the difficulties and challenges that many people experience. When Angelou died at the age of eighty-six, many famous and important black women, like Michelle Obama and Oprah Winfrey, spoke about how she had inspired them. And her words continue to matter and to inspire people to think carefully and understand more about the world and their place in it today.

7 Sabiha Gökçen

WORK
Pilot

PLACE
Türkiye

BORN
22nd March 1913

DIED
22nd March 2001

It is May 1935, and Sabiha Gökçen is standing on the edge of a large crowd at an air show in Türkiye. The air show is for the opening of a new flying school called the Türkkuşu or 'Turkish Bird' school. Some special planes without engines, called gliders, appear in the sky above. The gliders move silently across the sky, like big, strange birds. Young Sabiha stares up at them. She cannot believe her eyes. She has never seen anything like this and turns to the man next to her. Seeing her interest, he asks, 'Would you like to fly?' And she immediately replies that she is ready right now!

It was a very brave thing for Gökçen to say, because flying was still in its early days and there were frequent accidents, with pilots being injured or sometimes losing their lives in terrible crashes. Also, there were very few women pilots anywhere in the world then, and no woman in Türkiye had ever passed the test to become a pilot. But neither of these problems would stop the determined Gökçen. This brave, young woman went on to become Türkiye's first woman pilot. She also became the world's first woman fighter-plane pilot, and helped to inspire and train other women to become pilots, too.

Modern flying had started just over thirty years earlier in 1903, when the American Wright brothers had successfully built and flown a plane with an engine. Their first plane journey, or flight, was only twelve seconds, but it was a very special moment, because it showed the world that people could fly in planes. Other important flights soon followed. In 1909, there was the first flight from France to the UK, and ten years later, there was the first flight across the Atlantic.

By 1935, when Gökçen saw the glider planes at the air show, there had been big developments in how planes were designed and built, but flying was still difficult, dangerous, and uncomfortable. Many planes had no covers for the pilots, leaving them open to the wind, rain, and freezing temperatures. The noise from the engines was deafening, too. The planes were also heavy and hard to control at times, and the engines sometimes broke down suddenly. There were not many airports either, and pilots often had to land on rough fields in the middle of nowhere or even on beaches. Gökçen knew about these dangers, but she was also courageous, and desperately wanted to follow her dream.

Most of the pilots in the world at this time were men, but a small number of women had learned to fly, too. Two of the most famous were Amy Johnson from the UK and Amelia Earhart from the US. In 1930, Johnson had become the first woman to fly alone from the UK to Australia. And in 1935, Amelia Earhart had become the first person to make the 3,800-kilometre flight alone from the island of Hawaii to

California in the US. Ten people before her had died trying to make this long and dangerous flight.

Sabiha Gökçen was now about to join these fearless women in learning to fly. The man who had been standing next to Gökçen at the air show, and who had asked her if she would like to fly, was the Turkish president Kemal Atatürk. Gökçen had first met Atatürk ten years earlier when he was on a tour of Türkiye and had stopped in her hometown. Twelve-year-old Sabiha had bravely walked up to the president and spoken to him. She explained that she wanted to continue her education, although she was from a poor family and could not afford to study. The president invited her to continue her education in the Turkish capital, Ankara, along with some other children, and he became like a father to them. He also gave her the last name Gökçen – meaning 'of the sky'. It was the perfect name for a girl who would one day fall in love with flying.

Gökçen with Kemal Atatürk

After the air show, Atatürk spoke at once to the organizer of the show and said that Sabiha wanted to join the new flying school. Gökçen felt full of excitement about the plan and, at the age of only twenty-two, she became the first woman to train at the important Türkkuşu flying school. She worked hard and showed natural ability and, in a short time, she passed her test to fly a glider plane. Later in 1935, she was sent to Russia with seven other pilots – who were all men – to receive their higher-level glider training. Gökçen was an excellent glider pilot, and when she returned she was no longer just a pilot, but a glider trainer, too.

In 1936, Gökçen moved from the silent world of gliders to flying planes with engines, when she started training at a military flying school in the north-west of Türkiye. At that time, women were not usually allowed at military schools, and there was no military uniform for Gökçen to wear. So a special new uniform was designed and made just for her. After eleven months of training, she passed her pilot's test for planes with engines. She was the first woman ever to become a pilot in Türkiye.

Gökçen had already achieved so much, but she did not stop there. Her next step was to do full military flight training. It was difficult to learn to fly the heavy bomber or fighter planes, and she had to prepare for flying in dangerous air battles. But after training for long hours over six months, Gökçen became the world's first woman who was fully trained to fly military planes. With this new training, she flew in special military flights over the Aegean Sea, took part in her first fighter mission in 1937, and received a military flying medal for her work.

At this time, there was a danger of war both in Europe and in other parts of the world. The Turkish government

Gökçen flying a plane, May 1938

decided to plan a special tour around neighbouring countries in south-east Europe, which they said would send a message of peace to the world. For this very important mission, they chose one person – Sabiha Gökçen – to do a five-day tour of four countries by plane. She courageously accepted, although long-distance flights like this were full of dangers. Gökçen was going to be flying alone, finding the route by studying maps and then looking at the ground far below, following the line of the coast, rivers, and mountains.

Gökçen knew it would be a very tough journey, but on the 16th of June 1938, she sat in her plane at an airport in Istanbul, ready for the start of her peace mission. She perhaps felt a little worried, but also very excited at the thought of the flight ahead of her. A large group of reporters and photographers were waiting to watch her leave, and people from the government arrived to wish her success on this dangerous mission. As the crowd watched, Gökçen started the engine of her Vultee-V bomber plane. It began to move quickly along the ground and was soon high in the air over Istanbul.

Gökçen's flight started well, but after 150 kilometres, she suddenly flew into thick, grey cloud and extremely strong winds. She needed to act immediately, so she quickly changed her route to avoid the awful weather and managed to land safely near the Turkish town of Edremit. Her brave, quick thinking had saved her from a very dangerous situation and ensured that she could continue her mission. She then flew on to Athens, in Greece. After flying twice in a circle over the city, she landed perfectly and was welcomed by a crowd of important local people.

Reporters from newspapers and magazines across Europe wrote stories about the start of Gökçen's tour, as well as her next stops in the countries of Bulgaria, Yugoslavia, and Romania. At each place, she was met by large numbers of well-known local people, who all came to see this extraordinary woman pilot. At the end of her journey, Gökçen had flown three thousand kilometres alone across wide forests, high mountains, and deep valleys. And perhaps she had inspired other young women who read of her adventure to learn to fly, too.

Gökçen was now very well-known for her extraordinary abilities as a pilot, and she was asked to become the chief trainer at the Türkkuşu flying school. So, at the age of only twenty-six, Gökçen went to teach at the school where she had begun learning to fly just a few years earlier. At Türkkuşu, she taught hundreds of students, among them young Turkish women, who were desperate to follow Gökçen's brave example. Gökçen worked as the chief trainer at the Türkkuşu flying school until 1955. When she finally stopped working, she had done over eight thousand hours of flying, completed thirty-two military missions, and taught large numbers of men and women to fly.

Students at the Türkkuşu flying school, 1947

Gökçen is well known in Türkiye for her great achievements, and in 2001, a new airport was opened in Istanbul; it was called the Sabiha Gökçen International Airport. Gökçen sadly died some months later at the age of eighty-eight, but over her long life, this courageous woman was a wonderful example to young Turkish women, and she remains a very important person in the history of her country.

8 Miuccia Prada

WORK
Fashion designer

PLACE
Italy

BORN
10th May 1949

In 1984, everyone in the Italian fashion world was talking about a new designer 'must-have' bag. It was not like other expensive bags at the time, but if you had one of these bags, it showed that you had good style and money. It was not a shiny handbag, and it did not immediately look expensive. It was a simple, black backpack made from tough material with two useful pockets on the front, and it was for both men and women. It did have the name of the designer on it, but it was not written in big letters like many other designer bags in the 1980s.

1980's Prada 'must-have' bag

The bag was very innovative because, until that moment, backpacks had usually only been used by mountaineers, factory workers, or soldiers. In fact, the backpack's designer had got the idea for it from a visit to a factory which made things for the army. No one had seen a designer backpack before, and it challenged the central idea of what a designer bag could be. For the first time, people in the fashion world saw that there was a way to have a bag which was stylish and fashionable, but also really useful and simple. It was clear that the designer of this innovative bag did not like to 'follow the crowd'. But who was she – and how was she able to challenge stereotypes in fashion?

People soon learned that her name was Miuccia Prada, the granddaughter of Mario Prada. Mario had started the 'Prada' company in 1913 in Milan, Italy, making beautiful handbags, shoes, and luggage. Miuccia's mother later led the company, but Miuccia did not go into the family business when she finished school as people expected. Instead, she decided to go her own way and studied political science at Milan University, getting a higher-level degree in 1973.

A Prada store, Milan

During these years at university, Miuccia became very active in student politics. She was not afraid to openly challenge the ideas of the time, and she campaigned for greater equality between people at noisy protests on the streets of Milan. She became involved in the women's movement, too, and campaigned for gender equality. The idea that women should have the same rights as men became a very important part of her identity.

In 1970, while she was still at university, Miuccia joined the Prada business. Her mother decided to stop working for the company in 1978, and it was decided that Miuccia would now lead it. With her strong ideas about equality and her education in politics instead of business, she was perhaps an unlikely person to become the manager of this traditional family company. But Miuccia was determined to take this challenging next step in her life.

However, there was one difficulty: the Prada company had been successful in the past, but it was not doing at all well in the late 1970s. Prada's designs and way of doing business were moving too slowly for the modern world. The days of only selling traditional bags, shoes, or luggage were fast disappearing, and the company needed to change in order to survive. Miuccia understood these challenges and realized that she needed to be clever and innovative to make Prada successful again.

So, along with her future husband Patrizio Bertelli, Miuccia quickly began to change things at Prada. She was central to the management of the company and to developing new designs and ideas. It was at this time that she made the famous 1984 backpack which took the fashion world by surprise. It showed that Prada was changing and that Miuccia Prada was an innovative new designer.

In 1989, she proved this again, when she designed and introduced her first women's collection – a group of clothes for a season. Her designs were noticeable for their beautiful materials, simple shapes, and basic colours, and they were very popular. Miuccia was changing the fashion world with her new and interesting ideas, and the Prada business was becoming extremely successful again.

Miuccia in 1993

But Miuccia had even more new and exciting ideas for Prada. Her designs had become famous, but only very rich people could buy them. Miuccia wanted to design more affordable clothes and, after a lot of hard work, she introduced a new part of the Prada business. She called it 'Miu Miu', which was the name that Miuccia's friends and family called her. The first Miu Miu fashion show happened in Milan in 1993. Crowds of excited reporters sat waiting to see the new clothes, and they were not disappointed.

The collection was designed around one idea – the Wild West. Young women walked on stage wearing long skirts from the American west, with short coats and big boots. The clothes were fun, lively, and playful, and immediately everyone in the fashion world started talking about Miu Miu because it was fresh and new.

At that time, many other designers were making dresses which fitted closely to the body, with low necklines. These dresses could be uncomfortable to wear, and some people thought that women had to dress this way to be successful. However, Miuccia refused to conform to these ideas, and her designs helped to show that women could choose to dress differently if they wanted to. This was clearly shown by her famous Prada 1996 spring and summer show, which pushed against the gender stereotypes at the heart of the fashion business.

When the loud music began and the photographers started to take pictures, people could not believe their eyes. Most of the young women at this fashion show were not wearing the usual 'high fashion' clothes. They were walking down the long stage in sensible dresses, basic skirts, shorts, and everyday trousers. The colours of the collection were dull browns, boring greens, or unexciting blues, and some of the patterns looked old and boring. The women all had comfortable, flat shoes, too, which was very unusual in a fashion show.

The reporters began to whisper to each other – this is not a normal fashion show, is it? What were they seeing? It was the arrival of 'ugly fashion', and it was a very big and important moment. Miuccia later explained her ideas behind the clothes. 'Ugly is exciting. Ugliness is, to me, more interesting than the … idea of beauty. And why? Because ugly is human.'

Miuccia 'ugly' designs were innovative and stylish, and easy to wear, too. They sent the important message that women are free to wear whatever they want; they can feel good in their clothes, and still be fashionable and successful. Many other designers were inspired by these ideas, and the 'Prada style' became popular with the growing number of working women across the world, who could now achieve a strong, comfortable style in their workplace. Later, the more affordable clothes that women wore every day started to become less gender stereotyped, too, perhaps in part because of Miuccia's example.

A Miu Miu fashion show, 1996

The late 1990s were a very successful time for both Miuccia's designs and the Prada company. By 2001, the business had 307 shops across the world selling Prada clothes. Miuccia and her husband were very interested in how buildings looked, too, and they often asked internationally famous people to design their new shops. These buildings sometimes challenged the ideas behind traditional shops, in the same way that Miuccia's designs challenged stereotypes in women's fashion.

One of the most unusual shops is the Prada Epicenter in Tokyo, which was designed by Herzog & de Meuron and opened in 2003. Built on six floors, it is easily recognizable with 840 shiny, diamond-shaped pieces of glass on the outside. Everything inside feels modern and fresh, with echoes of the style of some of Miuccia's famous designs. Computer screens showing videos of the latest Prada clothes come down from the ceiling on long, white sticks, and the new collections look beautiful against the large, diamond windows behind them. Like most of the Prada shops around the world, the floor is partly covered in a black and white squared pattern.

The Prada Epicenter, Tokyo

The same special floor was also in the very first Prada shop in Milan. Today, visitors queue outside to see this traditional shop with its shiny, black and white stone floor, and its beautiful wooden and glass shelves showing bags or suitcases. They go there because it is a piece of fashion history, with Miuccia proving that a business which started over one hundred years ago can still be successful and innovative today.

From her early years as a student, to her many years as a famous designer, Miuccia Prada always refused to conform. She played an important part in giving women clothes that make them look *and* feel good, and challenged traditional thinking and gender stereotypes about what a woman should wear. For that, she has made a difference to women all over the world.

9 Clara Campoamor

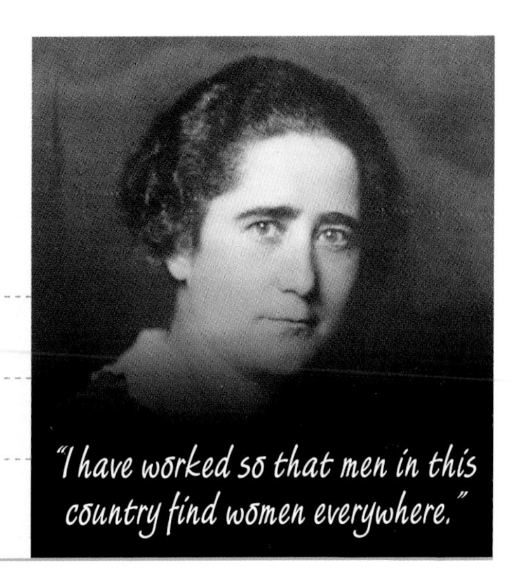

WORK
Women's rights campaigner

PLACE
Spain

BORN
12th February 1888

DIED
30th April 1972

When Clara Campoamor was growing up in Spain at the end of the nineteenth century, women did not have many of the basic rights that men had. They could not vote in elections and they received much lower pay for similar work. Married women were under their husband's control – for example, a married woman was not allowed to open a business, own a house, or change her address without the agreement of her husband. It was also extremely difficult for a woman to end her marriage by getting a divorce from her husband.

Many people believed that women were only supposed to get married, have children, and spend most of their time at home. This was not an unusual situation for women around the world at this time. So, when Campoamor was born in Madrid in 1888, it was expected that she would follow this same path. However, when Campoamor was only ten years old, her father died suddenly, leaving her mother to be the main earner for her young family. At the age of thirteen, Campoamor had to leave school in order to help her mother. This involved long hours of sewing and making clothes to earn money. She was left to read and study alone, disappointed that she could no longer be at school with her friends.

Although she had left education early, Campoamor was very intelligent and hard-working, and her natural abilities and careful planning helped her to become successful in her working life. From the age of twenty, she worked in government jobs in different parts of Spain, and in 1914, at the age of twenty-five, she came top in a special government exam. This allowed her to return home to Madrid as a teacher of secretaries in a government school for adults.

During this time, Campoamor frequently had more than one job, and one of these extra jobs came at an important moment in her life. After her return to Madrid, Campoamor found a job as a reporter on the newspaper *La Tribuna*. It was there that she became very interested in politics and women's rights, and she started to dream of equality for women in Spain. Soon, she was meeting other women from across the country who all wanted one thing – to change the lives of Spanish women by getting equality for women in all parts of the law and getting the right to vote. But how could they achieve this?

New Zealand had been the first country to give women the vote in 1893, and in the early twentieth century, women in other countries had begun to campaign for this right, too. In the late 1910s to early 1920s in India, a woman called Herabai Tata and her daughter Mithan Tata had organized a group to fight for women's right to vote, and they travelled far and wide trying to persuade people of their opinions.

A group of women in the UK called the Suffragettes had started a campaign in 1903, and this involved a variety of types of protest. Some street protests were peaceful, with people marching along and shouting 'Votes For Women!'. Others were more violent or extreme, with women breaking windows or locking themselves to government buildings.

Suffragettes protesting for the right to vote, 1912

Clara Campoamor decided to help to bring equality to Spain in a different way. In the 1920s, there were very few women lawyers in Spain, with the first woman only becoming a lawyer in 1922. All parts of the law were controlled by men, and it was sometimes difficult for women to find lawyers to work for them, to speak to lawyers in private, or to find the money to pay a lawyer. Campoamor quickly understood that if she became a lawyer, she could help these women herself.

Becoming a lawyer was going to be a long journey for Campoamor, who had not completed her early education and was not from a rich family who could help her. But she worked hard at evening classes to get the education that she needed. Sometimes, she had to do extra jobs to pay for the classes, too, but in only four years, she got a degree. Then she went to law school, and finally became a lawyer in 1924. She began to work, and in 1928 she became the first woman lawyer to appear in front of the most important judges in the country. It was an extraordinary achievement and the result of years of careful hard work, proving how determined she was to make a difference to the lives of other women in Spain.

In the late 1920s, Campoamor also opened her own law office in Madrid, where she used her understanding of the law to help other women. Her law office gave advice about family law, which involved marriage and divorce, as well as the treatment of children. Women who wanted a divorce often came to her, hoping to find help with their situation. She became so well-known that she worked on some of the most famous divorces of the time. She also started an international group for women in law, meeting other women lawyers from around the world.

In 1931, a new type of government in Spain introduced important changes in the law. Before, women had only been able to join political parties, but now they were able to stand for election to the Spanish Parliament, too, and they could become deputies at last. Campoamor realized that this was her chance to take another important step towards changing women's lives. She stood for election with her political group, the Radical Party, and was delighted to be successful. At the age of forty-three, she became one of only three women deputies in the Spanish Parliament.

Campoamor with the Radical Party, 1931

Later in 1931, Campoamor became part of a team of twenty-one deputies with a very important job. They had to prepare the new Spanish constitution – the ideas and laws that are used to organize a country. Campoamor fought hard for women's rights and helped to achieve gender equality in all parts of the constitution except for one – women still did not have the right to vote. Campoamor knew that she had to do more to achieve her most important goal.

Campoamor (left) working as a lawyer and a deputy

So, on the 1st of October 1931, Campoamor famously spoke to the Spanish Parliament. She was the first woman ever to speak there, and before she began, she looked at all the other deputies around her – there were 470 men and only one other woman. She looked down for a moment at the carefully prepared words in front of her, then she began to speak loudly and clearly about the desperate need for Spanish women to have the right to vote.

Over the years, Campoamor had developed a deep understanding of the law and excellent speaking abilities, and she was able to persuade others. At that moment, all of these things came together. As she spoke, she made clear arguments, gave important opinions, and asked challenging questions about why women should not be able to vote. 'How could Parliament begin to build a new government without half of the people in the country having the vote,' she asked determinedly, 'and don't women pay some of their money to the government in the same way as men?'

When Campoamor had finished speaking, many of the other deputies did not show their agreement or thank her. Instead, they said that women were not serious or responsible enough to have the right to vote. Even some men from her own political party agreed with these terrible ideas. But when the final moment came for the deputies to vote on this important question, the results were very clear. 188 deputies chose not to vote at all, 121 deputies voted against women having the vote, but most importantly, 161 deputies voted for women's right to vote!

Clara Campoamor had won the vote for women in her country. Of course, other people had played an important part in this moment too, but Campoamor's determined and endless work, as well as the unforgettable way that she spoke to the Spanish Parliament, had had a very decisive effect. On the 19th of November 1933, Campoamor finally achieved her dream when there were national elections to decide who would lead the country. In towns, cities, and villages across Spain, women stood in long queues, proudly waiting to vote for the first time. In many places, there were more women than men, with over six million women voting for the very first time.

A Spanish woman voting for the first time, 19th November 1933

As both a lawyer and a government deputy, Clara Campoamor made a truly important difference to women in her country. From early in her adult life, this very intelligent woman knew that she needed to spend many years studying, training, and working before she could help others. But she did not stop, always taking carefully planned steps towards equality for women, until she achieved her biggest goal. In helping to win the right to vote for women in Spain, Campoamor changed the lives of Spanish people and politics forever.

ability *(n)* something a person can do

achieve *(v)* to succeed in reaching a goal by working hard; **achievement** *(n)* a thing that somebody has done successfully

astronaut *(n)* a person whose job involves working in a spacecraft

beauty *(n)* the idea of being beautiful to look at

bid *(n)* an attempt to do something or to get something

campaign *(v & n)* to attempt to make changes in laws or communities, often with other people; **campaigner** *(n)* a person who campaigns

challenge *(v & n)* to question whether something is right or refuse to accept something; something difficult that tests a person's ability

champion *(n)* a person who is the best at a sport or a game; **championship** *(n)* an event to find the best in a sport

civil rights *(n)* the chance for every person living in a country to be treated the same by the law

climate *(n & adj)* the normal weather patterns of a place; **climate change** *(n)* changes to the climate because of human action; **climate emergency** *(n)* the idea that we must stop climate change quickly to save the Earth

committee *(n)* a group of people who are chosen, usually by a larger group, to decide things

community *(n)* a group of people who live or work in the same area, or are the same in some way

conform *(v)* to behave and think in the same way as most other people in a group

courage *(n)* the ability to do something dangerous, or frightening, without showing fear; **courageous** *(adj)* showing courage

culture *(n)* the way that people in a country or a group of people behave, and the art, food, and other things that they enjoy

degree *(n)* a student receives this when they have successfully completed university

deputy *(n)* the name for a politician in parliament in some countries

design *(n & v)* a drawing or plan from which something can be made; to decide how something will look, work, etc; **designer** *(n)* a person who designs things; **designer** *(adj)* something that is made by a designer

determined *(adj)* deciding to do something and refusing to stop until it is achieved; **determinedly** *(adv)* doing something in a determined way

Earth *(n)* this world; the planet that we live on

education *(n)* the teaching of a person at a school or university

election *(n)* the time when people choose a person or a group of people for a job, often in government, by voting; a person who wants the job must 'stand for election'

element *(n)* a simple, natural chemical material that is made of only one type of atom which cannot be broken into a simpler material

equality *(n)* when different groups of people have the same rights, life chances, and treatment as other groups; **inequality** *(n)* when a group of people has fewer rights than other groups

experiment *(n)* a test that you do to learn something or to see if something is true

explore *(v)* to travel around a new place to learn about it

eyebrow *(n)* the line of hair above the eye

fashion *(n & adj)* the business of making or selling clothes in new and different styles; a popular style of clothes, hair, etc.

figure skate *(n & v)* a type of ice skating in which you do jumps and turns; **figure skater** *(n)* a person who figure skates

gender *(n & adj)* being male or female, when thinking about how people behave or how they think of themselves, not biology

government *(n)* the group of people who control a country

identity *(n)* the feelings and beliefs that make people different from others

innovative *(adj)* introducing or using new ideas
inspire *(v)* to make somebody want to do something well
medal *(n)* A medal is usually round and made of metal; you get it when you do something very good, e.g. win a competition.
military *(adj & n)* connected with soldiers or the army
mission *(n)* an important trip, often for a special reason
movement *(n)* a group of people who share the same ideas or aims
parliament *(n)* the group of people who are chosen to make and change the laws of a country; the building where laws are made
physics *(n)* the science subject which studies energy and matter, e.g. heat, light, sound, electricity, and how things move
poetry *(n)* a type of writing; all types of poems
politics *(n)* the actions of governments and parliaments; being able to have an effect on the way a country or group is led; **politician** *(n)* a person whose job involves politics, as an elected member of parliament, etc.; **political** *(adj)* connected with government
protest *(n & v)* show a strong dislike of something through organized actions or words; **protester** *(n)* someone who protests
racism *(n)* any unfair or violent treatment of people because of their race
radioactive *(adj)* sending out very dangerous rays when the central parts of atoms are broken up; **radioactivity** *(n)* dangerous rays
ray *(n)* a narrow line of light, heat, or other energy
research *(n)* the careful study of a subject to discover new information about it; **researcher** *(n)* a person who researches
right *(n)* something that people can have and do by law
rink *(n)* a special flat floor of ice where you can figure skate
routine *(n)* planned movements which are made one after another, often as part of a dance or sport

self-portrait *(n)* a picture of the person who is making the picture
show *(n)* something that people go to see
space *(n & adj)* the place outside Earth, where the stars are
spacecraft *(n)* a vehicle that travels in space
stage *(n)* an area in a theatre or room which people stand on to say or show something
stereotype *(n)* an idea or picture that many people have in their heads of what a type of person or thing is like, which may not be true and may be harmful; **stereotypical** *(adj)* looking like and having the character that is expected from a certain type of person or thing
strike *(n & v)* to refuse to work or study as a way of showing that you strongly dislike something or want something to change
style *(n)* the way something is done or the way something looks
subject *(n)* a thing or person that is being discussed or described
traditional *(adj)* being part of the beliefs, culture, or way of life of a group of people that have not changed for a long time
treatment *(n)* something that is done to help someone to get better; a way of behaving towards another person
vote *(v & n)* a decision that you make in an election or at a meeting in order to choose somebody or decide something

Think Ahead

1 Look at the front and back cover of the book. Answer the questions.

1 The book is called *Women Who Made a Difference*. What do you think 'make a difference' means?

2 In which centuries did the different women in the book live?

3 Which countries did some of the women in the book come from?

4 What kind of people were all these women?

5 Which women do you recognize on the front cover?

2 Look at the contents page of the book. Answer the questions.

1 Which women in the book have you heard about?

2 What do you already know about these women?

3 What information would you like to learn about them? Why?

3 **RESEARCH Think of another world-famous woman who has made a difference. Find answers to these questions.**

1 When and where was she born?

2 What are five important facts about her life?

3 How could you describe her character?

4 Decide how you think she made a difference.

Chapter Check

INTRODUCTION Are the sentences true or false?

1 If someone makes a difference, they change people's lives and make the world a better place.

2 Each chapter of the book is about several women.

3 The book is about women because they have often had challenges which haven't been a problem for men.

4 Two of the women who appear in the book come from the same country.

5 There is nothing the same about the women's lives.

CHAPTER 1 Complete the sentences with the correct verbs. There is one verb that you do not need.

listened protested rose sailed spoke started stopped

1 On 20th of August 2018, Greta Thunberg ___________ to sit outside the Swedish Parliament building with her sign.

2 Thunberg's family agreed with her ideas about climate change, so they ___________ eating meat and flying by plane.

3 Many politicians around the world ___________ to Thunberg's warnings about climate change.

4 The number of Google searches about climate change ___________ because of the 'Greta effect'.

5 In September 2019, millions of people ___________ about the climate emergency in cities around the world.

6 On 23rd of September 2019, Thunberg ___________ to world leaders and climate specialists at the United Nations.

CHAPTER 2 **Answer the questions with numbers.**

1 How old was Mukai when Yuri Gagarin went into space?

2 How many people were killed on the shuttle *Challenger*?

3 How many times did Mukai go around the Earth on her first space mission?

4 How many times did Mukai go into space?

CHAPTER 3 **Choose the correct answers.**

1 The ideas from Marie Curie's work are...

a no longer used in everyday medicine.

b still used in modern medical treatments.

2 Marie Curie discovered radium and polonium...

a and separated both of them from pitchblende.

b but only separated radium from pitchblende.

3 The Curies had health problems because of the...

a freezing temperatures in their work room.

b effects of the element that they worked with.

4 To this day, Marie Curie is still the only person to...

a win the Nobel Prize in two different sciences.

b receive the Nobel Prize for physics twice.

CHAPTER 4 **Match the sentence halves.**

1 Kim first discovered the Olympics when she saw...

2 As a child, Kim was considered to be a future star by...

3 In 2011, Kim gave an excellent talk to...

4 Kim's success at the Vancouver Olympics inspired...

a the International Olympic Committee.

b new young skaters like You Young.

c international sportspeople on TV.

d her figure skating trainer.

CHAPTER 5 Complete each sentence with one word from the text.

1 Kahlo often challenged traditional s__________ of women in paintings.

2 When Kahlo was eighteen, she was in a c__________ which completely changed her life.

3 Kahlo loved the n__________ in her home country and often showed it in her paintings.

4 Kahlo went to her first art s__________ in her bed.

CHAPTER 6 Complete the sentences with the names of the people.

Martin Luther King Jr. *Maya Angelou*
Michelle Obama *Mrs Flowers* *Uncle Willie*

1 __________ helped Angelou to speak again.

2 As a child, __________ developed an extraordinary ability to look and listen, and remember things.

3 __________ was a very important leader of the civil rights movement in the US.

4 In the book *I Know Why the Caged Bird Sings*, __________ has to hide from the Ku Klux Klan.

5 When Angelou died, __________ said that she was a very inspiring person.

CHAPTER 7 Tick (✓) four true things about Sabiha Gökçen.

1 She was the first woman to fly from the UK to Australia.

2 She began to train as a pilot when she was twenty-two.

3 She became the first woman in the world who was fully trained to fly military planes.

4 She became the chief trainer at a top flying school.

5 An airport in Istanbul was named after her.

CHAPTER 8 Put the events in the life of Miuccia Prada and the Prada business in order.

a Miuccia Prada introduced the new idea of 'ugly fashion'.

b Mario Prada started the Prada business in Milan.

c Miuccia Prada started a new part of the Prada business which she called 'Miu Miu'.

d Miuccia Prada studied political science at Milan University and became interested in ideas about equality.

e Miuccia Prada became the manager of Prada.

CHAPTER 9 Correct the underlined words.

1 Campoamor decided to become a doctor in order to help the women of her country.

2 In the 1931 election, Campoamor became one of thirty women deputies in the Spanish Parliament.

3 Campoamor helped to write the Spanish national song.

4 Campoamor became the third woman to talk in front of the Spanish Parliament.

5 In the end, Campoamor won the right to divorce for the women of her country.

Focus on Vocabulary

1 Match the sentence halves.

1 If you *explore* somewhere, ...

2 If you *achieve* a goal, ...

3 If you *campaign* about something, ...

4 If you *vote*, ...

5 If you choose to *conform*, ...

a you succeed in doing it by working hard.

b you try to change it, often with other people.

c you help to choose a politician in an election.

d you behave in the same way as other people in a group.

e you travel around a new place to learn more about it.

2 Complete the sentences with the correct words.

ability courage deputy equality experiment movement

1 In the recent elections, our neighbour became a ___________ in the national parliament.

2 Scientists are doing a new ___________ for their research.

3 There's a ___________ which campaigns against climate change in our country.

4 My sister has the ___________ to swim well. She can swim fast and do long distances, too.

5 The government says that there needs to be more ___________ between men and women at work.

6 I could never go into space because I don't have the ___________ – I'd be too afraid.

Focus on Language

1 Complete the sentences with the past perfect continuous form of the verbs.

1 Greta Thunberg felt very tired on her arrival in New York because she __________ (travel) for days.

2 Chiaki Mukai __________ (wait) at home when she finally heard that she was going into space.

3 When Marie Curie came top of her physics class, she __________ (not study) science for very long.

4 Sabiha Gökçen __________ (not fly) for long when she suddenly came into some thick, dark clouds.

2 DECODE Read these sentences from the text. What do the prefixes and the suffixes mean? Match 1–5 to a–e.

1 Kahlo painted many <u>self</u>-portraits.
2 Kahlo's painting inspires us to <u>re</u>think what is beautiful.
3 She experienced life<u>long</u> pain.
4 The close<u>ness</u> between Kahlo and Fulang-Chang show her love of nature.
5 She painted in an <u>un</u>usual style.

a not
b showing a quality
c again
d related to yourself
e showing a length of time

3 DECODE Complete the text about Yuna Kim with the suffixes and prefixes from exercise 2.

At the Olympics, Yuna Kim looked [1]_____-confident, with no signs of nervous[2]_____ or [3]_____certainty. This was because she had done a week[4]-_____ practice with her trainer, [5]_____doing parts of her routine again and again.

Discussion

1 Read the sentences giving warnings. Which woman is the person in each sentence speaking to? Which warning is the strongest?

Chiaki Mukai Clara Campoamor Frida Kahlo
Marie Curie Miuccia Prada

1 I wouldn't go there to study. You can't speak the language very well.

2 Whatever you do, don't go to the opening of your new show. You're too ill.

3 I don't think you should apply to the programme. Look what happened on that recent mission.

4 Is it really a good idea to design 'ugly' clothes?

5 One thing I wouldn't do is speak to the Parliament. The deputies are nearly all men, and they won't listen to you.

2 THINK CRITICALLY Choose one of the women in exercise 1. Do you think she received this warning in real life? Why / Why not?

3 COMMUNICATE Work with a partner and choose one of these women. Write four warnings that people possibly gave her. Use the underlined words in exercise 1.

- Greta Thunberg
- Maya Angelou
- Sabiha Gökçen

4 With your partner, imagine how the women would reply to each of the warnings in exercise 3.

1 Read the encyclopaedia entry about another woman who made a difference.

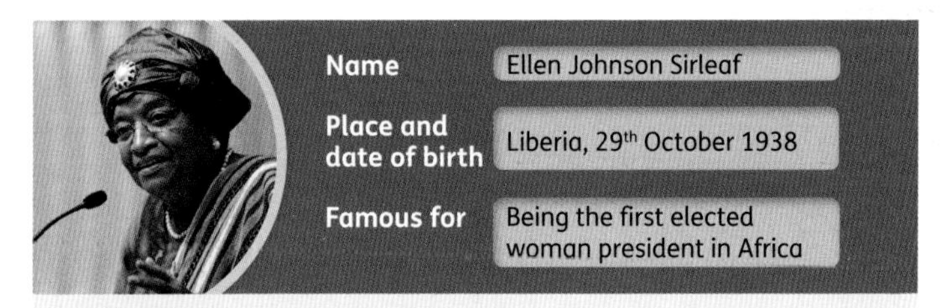

Earlier life

Johnson Sirleaf grew up in Monrovia, the capital of Liberia, and went to school there. Later, from 1961, she studied in the United States, and received a higher-level degree from Harvard – one of the top US universities.

Important moments

In 1971, Johnson Sirleaf returned to Liberia to work in important jobs in the government. However, she disagreed with the leaders of her country, and was put in prison twice. She then had to leave Liberia for twelve years in 1985 to avoid going to prison again. From 1989 to 2003, there were two wars in Liberia.

Johnson Sirleaf returned to her country in 1997, and became the President of Liberia in 2006. She was president until 2018, and she went on to work for the World Health Organization.

Achievements

As president, she kept the peace in Liberia after years of terrible war. She helped the lives of Liberian women, and also made the electricity better in towns and villages.

Prizes

She won the United States Presidential Medal of Freedom in 2007, and the Nobel Peace Prize in 2011, as well as many other prizes.

Famous quote

'To girls and women everywhere, I (give you) a simple invitation. My sisters, my daughters, my friends; find your voice.'

2 **In which part of the encyclopaedia entry on page 90 can you find the answers to these questions about Ellen Johnson Sirleaf?**

1 What did she say to inspire others?

2 What were some of the important times in her life?

3 Where and when was she born?

4 Why is she famous?

5 What particular things has she achieved?

6 What has she won?

7 What did she do in her younger years?

3 **Choose a woman who has made a difference from your country or part of the world. Put the questions in exercise 2 in the correct order. Find the answers to the questions about your chosen woman.**

4 CREATE **Use your answers in exercise 3 to write an encyclopaedia entry similar to the information in exercise 1.**

5 COMMUNICATE **Work with a partner. Ask your partner the questions in exercise 2 and find out more about their chosen woman.**

If you liked this Bookworm, why not try...

Gandhi

LEVEL 4
Rowena Akinyemi

Who will speak for the poor? Who will listen to slaves, and those who have no rights? Who will work for a future where everyone is equal?

'I will,' said Mohandas Gandhi. And he began to fight in a way the world had not seen before – not with weapons and words of hate, but with the power of non-violence. This is the story of a man who became the Father of the Nation in his own country of India, and great leader for the whole world.

Nelson Mandela

LEVEL 4
Rowena Akinyemi

In 1918 in the peaceful province of Transkei, South Africa, the Mandela family gave their new baby son the name Rolihlahla – 'troublemaker'. But the young boy's early years were happy ones, and he grew up to be a good student and an enthusiastic sportsperson.

Who could imagine then what was waiting for Nelson Mandela – the tireless struggle for human rights, the long years in prison, the happiness and sadness of family life, and one day the title of President of South Africa?
